英訳付き
伝承折り紙帖

Origami Booklet

Traditional Edition

監修／小林一夫

Editorial Supervisor
Kazuo Kobayashi

はじめに

受け継がれてきた日本の心

奴さんや紙相撲で遊んだ楽しさ。初めて折り鶴やきれいな花ができあがったときの嬉しさ。——日本人の多くはそうした記憶を持っているはずです。

伝承とは伝え聞くことであり、世代から世代へと受け継がれていくこと。信仰・風習・言い伝えなどと同じく、折り紙も伝承によって普及し、その数百年の歴史をいまに伝えています。折り紙の原形は宗教的・儀礼的なものとされ、古来、結納や結婚式の祝儀などの包みには、紙で折った鶴がどこかについていました。そのおめでたい鶴が、包みから離れて単独に折られ、女性や子どもの楽しみ、遊びとして広まったのが「遊戯折り紙」の始まりといわれています。

二次元の平らな世界（紙）を、鳥や生きもの、包みや入れもの、花、舟など三次元の立体に折り上げ、遊びや実用として暮らしに活かすのは日本人特有の感性でしょう。本書の江戸千代紙に見られる文様もまた、長い歴史のなかで日本人の感性と美意識が創り出したものです。英訳が付くことによって、日本の伝統的な折り紙と文様を、広く世界の人々へ伝えることができたら幸いです。

国際おりがみ協会理事長　小林一夫

Introduction

From Mother to Child: The Spirit of Japan

Good times playing with paper *yakko-san* (footmen) or sumo wrestlers, the elation of folding a paper crane or a pretty flower for the first time — most Japanese people have such memories.

Oral traditions are passed from generation to generation by word of mouth. Origami spread through oral tradition in the same way as beliefs, customs and legends, and brings hundreds of years of history to the present day. Original origami forms had religious and formal significance, and folded paper cranes have long been used to decorate fancy envelopes used to hold wedding and engagement gift money. It seems that "recreational origami" came about when these celebratory cranes were detached from envelopes and made on their own, soon becoming a delightful pastime for women and children.

The Japanese have a particular sensibility that allowed them to turn the two-dimensional, flat world of paper into three-dimensional objects such as birds, animals, fancy envelopes, boxes, flowers and boats, and make use of them for both play and practical purposes in day-to-day life. The patterns found on the *edo chiyogami* in this book were also created over many years through the sensibilities and awareness of beauty of the Japanese people. With the English translation in this book, I hope the traditional origami and patterns of Japan will be passed on to people around the world.

K. Kobayashi

Kazuo Kobayashi
The Chairman of the International Origami Association

Contents

足付き三方
Sanbo

裏梅 Ura-ume

奴さん
Yakko-san

狂言家紋 Kyogen-kamon

袴
Hakama

亀甲松 Kikko-matsu

手裏剣
Shuriken

紗綾形 Sayagata

鳩
Dove

桜花 Ohka

椿
Camellia

蝶紗綾 Cho-saya

相撲取り
Sumo Wrestler

子持吉原 Komochi-yoshiwara

41

渡し舟
Ferryboat

大網格子 O-ami Goshi

43

ピアノ
Piano

市松 Ichimatsu

45

燕
Swallow

七宝 Shippo

47

祝い包み
Iwai-zutsumi

扇面鮫小紋 Senmen Samekomon

49

鷹
Hawk

藤花 Tohka

51

提灯
Chochin

雲立涌 Kumo-tatewaku

53

蝸牛
Snail

観世波 Kanze-nami

55

蝉
Cicada

麻の葉 Asanoha

57

豚
Pig

棒縞 Bojima

59

帽子
Hat (Sombrero)

蝶の舞 Cho no Mai

61

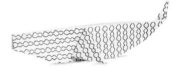

鯨
Whale

瓢箪立涌 Hyotan-tatewaku

63

折り方 How to Fold the Models

日本の伝承折り紙

　日本の「折り紙」には、三百年以上の長い歴史があります。江戸時代の1680年には、蝶の形の折り紙（婚礼などの席で飾る「雄蝶・雌蝶」）の記録が見られ、およそ二百年前には、さまざまな鶴の折り方を書いた『千羽鶴折形』という世界最古の折り紙の本が出版されています。「伝承折り紙」とは、こうした折り紙の長い歴史の中で生まれ、人々に親しまれながら、親から子へ、手から手へと、時代を超えて伝え継がれてきた作品のことをさします。いつどこで、だれが最初に考案したのかはわかりませんが、その形には、日本の風土や文化、また日本人の美的感性が反映されています。

　本書で紹介するのはそのほんの一部で、「奴さん」「手裏剣」など、いまでも子どもたちになじみの深いものから、「御駕篭」「狐の面」「お化け」など、最近はあまり目にすることのない作品、「花たとう」「祝い包み」など、日本古来の“包む文化”とも関わる作品など、24点を集めています。伝承作品は、時代を経るごとに名前や折り方が変わっていくものもあり、新しい創作折り紙のベースになることもあります。たとえば本書に掲載したソンブレロ型の「帽子」は、かつては「荷舟」（荷物をのせた小舟）と呼ばれたものが原形で、また「ピアノ」は「家」や「狐の面」の折り方から発展したものです。

　日本の伝統文様が彩る美しい江戸千代紙で、一点一点折り紙を作ってみてください。

　一枚の紙から生まれる創造の世界。伝承折り紙は、それぞれが「小さな古典」としていまに伝えられてきているのです。

About Traditional Japanese Origami

Japanese origami has a long history of over three hundred years. In the year 1680 of the Edo era, records of butterfly-shaped models (such as the *ocho* [male] and *mecho* [female] butterflies displayed at wedding ceremonies) appeared. Then, nearly two hundred years ago, *Senbazuru Orikata*, a book describing a variety of ways to fold paper cranes and the oldest origami book in the world, was published. Thus was the tradition of making origami born. Origami has been enjoyed and passed down from parent to child and from hand to hand through the ages. It is not known when, where or by whom origami was first devised, but in its shapes, the climate and culture of Japan and the aesthetic sensibilities of the Japanese people are reflected.

Just twenty-four models, a small fraction of the total, are introduced in this book: from models children today are still familiar with, such as the *yakko-san* and the ninja star, to models that are not often seen recently, such as the palanquin, the fox mask and the ghost, to models related to Japan's culture of wrapping things, such as the *hana-tato* and the *iwai-zutsumi*. Names and methods of folding occasionally change with the passage of ages, and at times traditional models are used to create new models. For example, the sombrero hat that appears in this book was originally a traditional cargoboat model, and the piano was developed from the house and the foxmask model.

Please try making these models with the traditionally patterned and beautiful *edo chiyogami* provided.

You will discover a world of creativity in each sheet of paper. These traditional origami models are "tiny classics" that have been passed down to the present day.

この本の使い方
Using This Book

この本の千代紙を使って、
24種類の折り紙作品がつくれます。
また、それぞれの紙の説明によって
日本の伝統文様について知ることができます。

You can make 24 origami models with
the *chiyogami* paper found in this book.
You will also learn about traditional
Japanese patterns from the explanations
that accompany each paper.

古いもののよさを
楽しんでね
We hope you enjoy
these traditional
models!

1 つくりたい作品を選びます。
Choose a model you would like to make.

2 ミシン線に合わせて紙をカットします。
ミシン線にいちど折り目をつけてからカットするときれいに切り取ることができます。
Cut the paper along the perforated line.
In order to cut the paper neatly, first make a crease along the perforated line.

3 折り方の載っているページを開きます。　例) see page 66
Open to the "How to Fold" page for your model. See page 66 for an example.

4 折り図を見ながら番号順に折っていきます。
完成した作品は、見本の写真と同じ位置に図柄（文様）が見えるとは限りません。
Look at the diagrams and fold in order.
On your completed models, the patterns will not necessarily appear
in the same position as in the sample photos.

5 できあがったら、好きな場所に飾ったり、友だちにプレゼントしましょう。
After you have finished, you can display your creation anywhere you please
or give it to a friend as a present.

6 折り方がわかったら、ほかの紙でも折ってみましょう。好きな色や柄、
いろいろな大きさの紙でつくってみると、さらに折り紙の楽しさが広がります。
Once you have got the idea, try making the model with different kinds of paper.
You can enjoy making these origami models again and again using different
sized papers of your favorite colors and designs.

この本で使う記号の意味
The Symbols Used in This Book

線の種類や矢印など、この本で使う記号の説明をします。
折り図を見るときに必要になるので記号の意味を覚えましょう。

Here we will explain the symbols used in this book, including the different folding lines and arrow marks. These symbols will help you understand the diagrams, so please remember them.

谷折り Valley fold (dashed line)

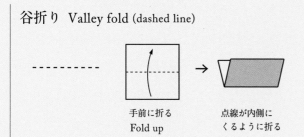

手前に折る
Fold up

点線が内側に
くるように折る

折りすじをつける Make a crease (fold and unfold)

いちど折って線をつけたあと、紙をもどす

山折り Mountain fold (dashed-dotted line)

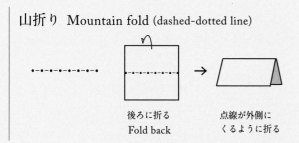

後ろに折る
Fold back

点線が外側に
くるように折る

矢印の方向に折る Fold in the direction of the arrows

The Symbols Used in This Book

紙の向きを変える Rotate

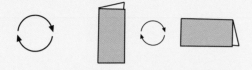

はさみを使う Use scissors

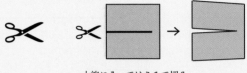

太線にそってはさみで切る
Cut along the thick line.

うらがえす Turn over

上下の位置は変えない
Do not change the orientation of the top and bottom.

紙のあいだを開く Insert fingers and open

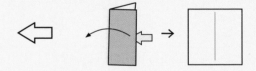

図を拡大する Enlargement

 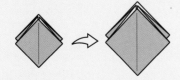

同じ幅・同じ角度 Same width, same angle

基本の折り方
Basic Folds

よく使う折り方です。とくに「四角折り」や「中わり折り」はよく使います。
These are the most common folds, especially the square base and the inside reverse fold.

四角折り Square base

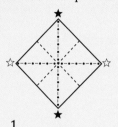

1
谷線、山線の折りすじ
をつける
Make valley and mountain
creases as shown.

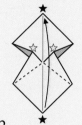

2
★と★、☆と☆がつく
ようにたたむ
Fold to bring the matching
star points together.

3
できあがり
Finished!

中わり折り Inside reverse fold

1
折りすじをつける
Make a crease as
shown.

2
紙のさきを、内側に入
れるように折る
Push the point between
the layers and fold in.

3
できあがり
Finished!

かぶせ折り Outside reverse fold

1
折りすじをつける
Make a crease as
shown.

2
紙を上にかぶせるよう
に折る
Fold the paper over
as shown.

3
できあがり
Finished!

Basic Folds

凧折り Kite base

1
半分に折って折りすじ
をつける
Fold in half (make a
valley crease).

2
真ん中の線まで折る
Fold both edges to
the centerline.

3
できあがり
Finished!

かんのん折り Kannon fold

1
半分に折って折りすじ
をつける
Fold in half (make a
valley crease).

2
真ん中の線まで折る
Fold both edges to
the centerline.

3
できあがり
Finished!

ざぶとん折り Blintz base

1
中心をつくる
Make a center point.

2
4つのかどを中心に向
かって折る
Fold all four corners to
the center.

3
できあがり
Finished!

※中心のしるしのつけ方
How to make the center point:

軽く半分に折って、真ん中をおさ
えてもどす。別の向きから軽く半
分に折って、真ん中をおさえても
どす→×印がついたところが紙の
中心
Fold the paper in half lightly
and pinch the center, then
open. Repeat from the opposite
direction. The resulting cross
mark is the center point.

足付き三方
さん ぼう

Sanbo : Four-legged Box

三方とは神様への供え物をのせる
入れもののこと。これは足を付け
て少し中国風にアレンジされてい
ます。

A *sanbo* is a container used to
hold offerings for the gods. This
one has legs and is arranged in a
somewhat Chinese style.

see page 66

裏梅

Ura-ume:Upside-down Ume Blossoms

梅は古くから日本人に愛された花で、文様の種類も数多くあります。これは梅の花を裏や横から見たようすを図案化しているため「裏梅」と呼ばれています。

Ume (Japanese plum tree) blossoms have long been loved by the Japanese, and there is a wide assortment of *ume* motifs. Because this pattern shows stylized *ume* flowers from the back and sides, it is called *ura-ume* (upside-down *ume*).

袴
はかま

Haka

おもに是
服で、い
ような
奴さん

These
Japanes
usually
old day
with th
models

奴さん
Yakko-san

半纏を着た上半身をかたどった折
はんてん
り紙です。奴さんは武家の使用人
のことで、大名行列では毛槍をか
ざして先頭を歩きました。

This model represents the upper
half of a *yakko-san* wearing
a short coat. *Yakko-san* were
servants of the samurai, and in
daimyo processions they would
march at the front waving
feathered lances called *keyari*.
(*Daimyo* were powerful feudal barons.)

see page   see page 68

紗綾形
Sayagata

卍の形を崩して連続させた文様で「卍
崩し」または「卍つなぎ」ともいいます。
桃山～江戸時代に明（中国）から輸入
された織物（紗綾）の地紋に使われて
いたためこの名が付いています。
（卍は仏教では仏の体に表れた瑞兆の印）

This pattern of broken and
interconnected *manji* 卍 shapes
may also be called *manji-kuzushi*
or *manji-tsunagi*. It was named
sayagata because it appeared in the
weave of textiles (*saya*) imported
during the Momoyama and Edo
eras from Ming China.
(The *manji* 卍 mark is a sign of good
fortune that appeared on the body of the
Buddha.)

鳩
Dove

飛んでいる鳩の折り紙です。鳩は
昔、「八幡さま」などの神社で神聖
な生き物とされ、いまも各地の神
社や公園でたくさん見られます。

This is a flying dove. In the
past, the dove was considered
to be a sacred creature at
shrines such as those of the god
Hachiman. They can still be
found in abundance at shrines
and parks throughout Japan.

see page 71

桜花

Ohka : Cherry Blossom

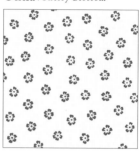

桜の花弁を素朴にデザイン化した文様
です。桜は日本古来の花で、国花でも
あります。平安時代から貴族を中心に
愛好され、江戸時代にはいまのような
「お花見」の風習が庶民に広まりました。

This is a pattern of simply stylized
sakura (cherry blossom) petals. The
sakura has long held importance
in Japan, and is Japan's national
flower. In the Heian era, the
aristocracy developed a fondness
for it. In the Edo era the custom of
hanami (cherry-blossom viewing),
which is still enjoyed today, spread
among the populace.

椿
Camellia

「椿」は字の通り春を告げる木で、冬から早春に赤や白の花をつけます。日本では地面に落ちた花も「落ち椿」といって風流を楽しみます。

The kanji character for *tsubaki* (椿) is a combination of the characters for tree (木) and spring (春). True to its name, this tree announces the arrival of spring with early red and white blossoms. In Japan, blossoms that have fallen on the ground are called *ochi-tsubaki*, and their elegance is a delight.

see page 72

蝶紗綾

Cho-saya：Butterflies on Sayagata

「紗綾形」の地に、二頭の蝶が向かい合う「向蝶」の文様が描かれています。「向蝶」は昔の公家や位の高い人々だけが用いた「有職文様」の一つで、家紋にも見られます。

Two dancing butterflies face each other, forming circles, on a *sayagata* background. *Mukai-cho* (facing butterflies) is a court pattern that was used exclusively by court nobles and those of high rank, sometimes as a family crest.

菖蒲
あやめ

Ayame : Iris

高貴な色とされる紫の花が昔から
愛され、同じ仲間の燕子花（かき
つばた）とともに日本画によく描
かれています。初夏の代表的な花
です。

This regal purple flower is an
old-time favorite, and is often
depicted in traditional Japanese
paintings, along with another
kind of iris, the *kakitsubata*. It
represents early summer.

see page 74

泪鹿の子

Namida-kanoko: Teardrop Kanoko

鹿の体毛の白い斑点のような細かい連続文様を「鹿の子」といいます。これはそのバリエーションの一つで、白い部分が涙のしずくのように見えるのでこの名が付いています。

Continuous patterns of fine white spots like those on the coat of a deer are called *kanoko*. This variation was given the name *namida-kanako* because its white spots resemble teardrops (*namida*).

御駕篭
おかご

Okago : Palanquin

昔の乗り物で、木や竹でできた駕
篭に人が乗り、前後の棒を人がか
ついで運びました。もともとは身
分の高い人の移動用です。

This is an old-world form of
transportation. A person would
ride in the wood or bamboo
box of the palanquin, which
was carried by men holding the
front and back poles. It was
originally used by those of high
rank when they went out and
about.

see page 76

花菱
Hanabishi : Flower Chestnut

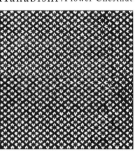

花びらを単純化して菱形に連続させた
文様です。菱（沼や池の水草で種子が
菱形をしている）の形をモチーフにし
た幾何文様は古代から見られ、庶民の
着物の柄にも人気がありました。

A pattern of simplified flower
petals connected in diamond
shapes like water chestnuts. Motifs
of the diamond-shaped seeds of
the water chestnut (a plant found
in marshes and ponds) have been
seen in geometrical patterns since
ancient times, and were once
popular on the kimonos of the
common people.

狐の面
きつね

Fox Mask

後ろから上下に指を入れて、ぱく
ぱくさせて遊ぶ折り紙です。狐は
日本では神社の使いともされ、昔
話や童話にもよく登場します。

Insert your fingers in both the
top and bottom from the back
to make your fox open and close
her mouth. In Japan, the fox
is said to be a servant of the
shrines, and often appears in
folktales and nursery rhymes.

see page 79

鮫青海波

Same-seigaiha : Sharkskin Waves

海の波のように半円形の曲線を重ねて
いく文様を「青海波」といいます。こ
れは鮫皮のような「鮫小紋」の点々で
波を描くため「鮫青海波」。着物地に
も使われる文様です。

Patterns of half-circles overlapping
like the waves of the ocean
are called *seigaiha* (wave crest
patterns). Here, the waves are
drawn in dots like those of the
common sharkskin pattern, so this
is called *same* (shark) *seigaiha*. This
pattern is sometimes found on
kimono fabrics.

お化け

Obake : Ghost

日本のお化け（幽霊）は足先が見
えず、宙に浮いて見えるのが特徴。
妖怪や怪物とは違い、うらみや哀
しみを抱いてこの世に現れます。

A special characteristic of
Japanese spooks and ghosts is
that they have no feet and seem
to float in the air. They differ
from phantoms and monsters in
that they haunt this world out
of spite or grief.

see page 80

豆絞り

Mameshibori : Mini Tie-dye

細かな点を並べた文様で手ぬぐいによく見られ、お祭りのハチマキもこの柄が代表的です。豆は「小さい」という意味で、昔は大変手間のかかる「絞り」の技法で染めていました。

This pattern of fine dots in rows is often seen on towels and is also a typical pattern on festival headbands. *Mame* means both "bean" and "mini." In earlier times, this design was made using an extremely time-consuming tie-dye technique.

雉
きじ

Kiji : Pheasant

日本の国鳥で、オスは青緑色を
ベースにした多彩な羽毛と長い尾
をもっています。折るときも尾を
シャープに仕上げるときれいです。

The pheasant is the national
bird of Japan. The male bird has
iridescent blue-green feathers
and a long tail. This model
looks best when the tail is
folded sharply.

see page 81

大納言
Dainagon : Great Councilor

「大納言」とは昔の朝廷の官位で、左大臣、右大臣、内大臣に次ぐ高い位でした。花菱を草が丸く囲むこの文様は、糸を浮かせて文様を織りだす「浮線綾文」の一つで、大納言など高位の人が用いた有職文様です。

Dainagon, or great councilor, was a high official rank of the old Imperial Court, just below the top three ministers. With flowers encircled by grasses, this pattern is one of the fusenryo patterns that were made in relief with raised threads, and was a court pattern used by those of high rank such as the dainagon.

相撲取り
Sumo Wrestler

日本の国技「相撲」の力士の折り
紙です。二つ作って紙箱などの台
におき、台をトントン叩いて競わ
せて遊びます（「紙相撲」という）。

This is a sumo wrestler. Sumo
is Japan's national sport. If
you make two and put them
on a base such as a board, you
can then make them fight by
tapping the board (this is known
as "paper sumo").

see page 82

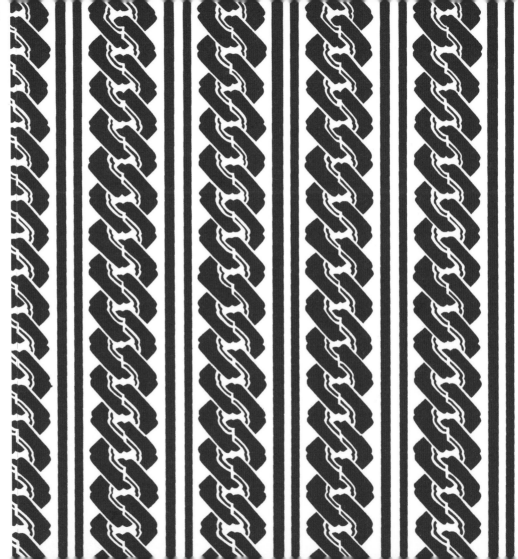

子持吉原
Komochi-yoshiwara

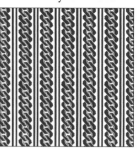

昔、遊郭のあった吉原の茶屋の暖簾や
男衆の浴衣などに用いられた「吉原つ
なぎ」という文様。内側に細い線で二
重に描かれているのを親子に見立てて
「子持吉原」と呼びます。

In the old days, the *yoshiwara-tsunagi* pattern was often used for the *noren* (door curtains) of teahouses in the licensed quarters of Yoshiwara and for men's cotton summer kimonos. Drawn in double with a thin inner line, this pattern resembles a parent with a child, and so came to be called *komochi-yoshiwara* (*yoshiwara* with child).

渡し舟
Ferryboat

人を乗せて川を往復する木舟を模した折り紙です。アジア各地ではサンパン船と呼ばれます。水に浮かべて遊べますよ。

This model imitates a wooden boat used to carry people back and forth across rivers. It is known as a "sampan" throughout Asia. You can actually float it on the water!

see page 83

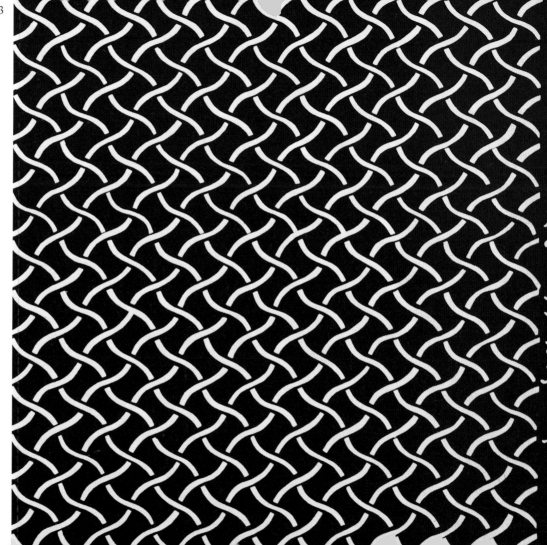

大網格子
O-ami Goshi : Big Net Checks

線が交差している連続文様を「格子」
といいます。これは太くしっかり編ま
れた「網」をモチーフにしているので
「大網格子」です。

Continuous patterns of intersecting
lines are called *koshi* (checked)
patterns. This motif of a thick
and tightly woven net is called
o-ami goshi (big net checks).

ピアノ
Piano

もとは伝承の「お家」の折り方から生まれたアップライト型ピアノの折り紙です。鍵盤を書いたらソナタが弾けそうです♪

This upright piano was designed from a traditional house model. When a keyboard is drawn on, it seems as though one could play a sonata.

see pages 84

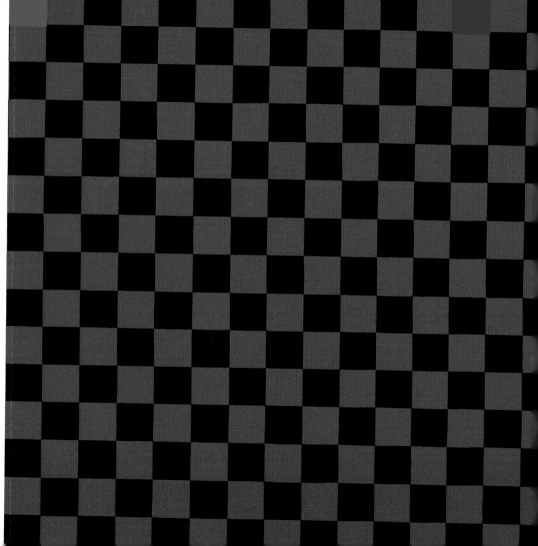

市松

Ichimatsu : Stone Pavement

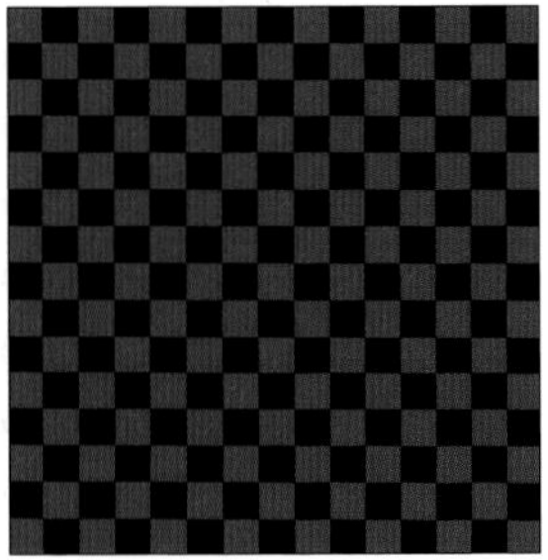

世界各地で古くから見られるシンプルな文様です。日本では「石畳」と呼ばれていましたが、江戸時代に佐野川市松という人気役者が袴に用いたところ大流行し、「市松文様」と呼ぶようになりました。

This is a simple pattern that has long been seen around the world. In Japan, it was once called *ishidatami* (stone pavement), but has been known as the *ichimatsu* pattern ever since the Edo era, when it became very fashionable after the popular actor Ichimatsu Sanogawa used it for his *hakama* (pants).

<ruby>燕<rt>つばめ</rt></ruby>

Swallow

春にやってくる鳥です。空中で虫を食べるため「ツバメ返し」と呼ばれる独特の飛び方をします。燕尾服のようにおしゃれに折りましょう。

The swallow appears in spring. Because it catches insects in midair, it has a special way of flying know as the *tsubame-gaeshi* (swallow crisscross). Give him a fancy fold like a swallow-tailed coat.

see page 84

七宝

Shippo : Seven Treasures

円をつなぐ「七宝つなぎ」(32ページ参照) をさらに単純化した文様です。「七宝」 とは仏教でいう七つの宝石類をさしま すが、文様が四方八方へ無限に広がる ことから、音の似ている「七宝」の名 をあてたようです。

This is a simplification of the interconnected circles of the *shippo-tsunagi* pattern (see page 32). The word *shippo* indicates the seven jewels of Buddhism. This pattern seems to have been given the name *shippo* because *shippo* sounds like *shiho-happo*, which means "in all directions."

祝い包み
Iwai-zutsumi:
Celebratory Wrapping

お祝いのお金を包む「折り形」の
一つで、鶴が慶賀を表します。格
式の高い家に伝わる「礼法」では、
包みの折り方にさまざまな決まり
ごとがありました。

This is a method of folding
paper to wrap money for
celebrations. The crane expresses
congratulations. Among the upper
classes, there were once detailed
rules of etiquette concerning the
folding of wrappings.

see page 86

扇面鮫小紋
Senmen Samekomon : Sharkskin Fans

点々で描いた「麻の葉」「青海波」「紗綾形」などの文様を一枚の中で扇形に組み合わせています。吉祥文様を合わせることでさらに「めでたさ」を強調するという意味もあります。

Here, patterns such as hemp-leaves, waves and *sayagata* are drawn in dots and arranged in fan shapes on one sheet. In combining these auspicious motifs, happiness is even further emphasized.

<ruby>鷹<rt>たか</rt></ruby>
Hawk

鷹は太くて鋭い脚の爪をもち、狩りが得意。昔の武将や大名たちは、調教した鷹を使って獲物をとらせる「鷹狩り」を好みました。

The hawk is a bird with long, sharp talons that is very good at hunting. In the past, generals and *daimyo* enjoyed *taka-gari*, or hunting with trained hawks that could catch prey.

see page 88

藤花

Tohka : Wisteria Flowers

藤は、「藤色」といわれる薄紫の房状の花が古くから愛されてきました。平安時代後期に藤原氏一族が繁栄したのを機に、その姓名の由来である「藤の花」の文様が広く用いられるようになったそうです。

The bunched light-purple flowers of the wisteria, or *fuji*, have long been loved. In the latter half of the Heian era, the Fujiwara clan flourished and patterns of *fuji* flowers, for which the Fujiwaras were named, came to be widely used.

ちょうちん
提灯
Chochin : Paper Lantern

木や竹ひごの枠に紙を貼り、中に
ろうそくを灯す伝統的な照明具で
す。折り畳んで携帯もでき、懐中
電灯の代わりもしました。

This is a traditional lantern that
consists of a thin, paper-covered
wood or bamboo frame with
a lit candle inside. It can be
folded up and carried, and was
used much like a flashlight.

see page 90

観世波

Kanze-nami : Kanze Waves

能の宗家・観世家が装束に用いたことから「観世波」や「観世水」と呼ぶ文様です。流れる水や水面のゆらめきまで文様化して表現する感性は、日本人独特のものでしょう。

This pattern is called *kanze-nami* (waves) or *kanze-mizu* (water) because it was used for the costumes of the head family of Noh, the Kanze family. The sensibility to make patterns of things such as flowing water or ripples must be a unique trait of the Japanese.

蟬
せみ

Cicada

蟬の声は夏の風物詩。林などでたくさんの蟬がいっせいに鳴くのを「蟬時雨」といいます。小さな目を折るのがポイントです。
せみ しぐれ

The song of the cicada is a feature of summer. Many cicadas singing all at once in the forest are called *semi-shigure* (cicada showers). Try to make his eyes very small.

see page 92

麻の葉
Asanoha : Hemp Leaves

麻の葉を図案化した文様で、麻は丈夫
でまっすぐ成長することから赤ん坊の
産着にもよく用いられます。魔除けの
意味もあり、浮世絵を見ると当時の庶
民の着物に「麻の葉」が大変多く用い
られていたことがわかります。

This stylized pattern of hemp leaves
is often used for baby clothing
because hemp is strong and grows
straight. It also said to ward off evil
spirits. If you look at ukiyo-e pictures,
you will see that *asanoha* (hemp leaf)
patterns were once very often used for
the kimonos of commoners.

豚
Pig

日本の絵本やアニメにもよく登場
し、子どもたちに人気の動物です。
先祖のイノシシの子は「瓜坊」と
呼ばれて親しまれています。

The pig often appears in
Japanese picture books and
anime, and is a popular animal
with children. The piglets of
the wild boar, an ancestor of
the pig, are lovingly called *uribo*
(little melons).

see page 93

棒縞

Bojima : Bar Stripes

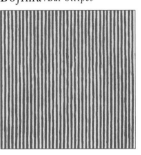

太い縦縞を「棒縞」といいます。江戸
時代に南蛮貿易で入ってきた綿布には、
日本では珍しい縦縞柄があり、それを
南方の島から来た「島もの」と呼んだ
のが「縞」の語源。江戸時代後期には
粋な縦縞の着物が大流行しました。

Thick vertical stripes are called *bojima*.
There were vertical stripes, which wer
rare in Japan, on cotton fabrics that
were imported from Southeast Asia in
the Edo era. Since they came from the
southern islands, these were called *shin
mono* (island things). This is how strip
came to be called *shima*, which means
both stripe and island. In the latter ha
of the Edo era, stylish vertically stripe
kimonos were extremely popular.

帽子
Hat (Sombrero)

伝承折り紙の「荷舟」が、南米の
つば広帽子になりました。新聞紙
くらいの大きな紙で折れば、実際
にかぶって遊べます。

This wide sombrero from South
America was designed from a
traditional cargo-boat model.
If you make it from a sheet of
newspaper, you can actually
wear it!

see page 94

蝶の舞
Cho no Mai : Butterfly Dance

蝶の文様は七世紀に中国から伝来し、平安時代には公家の装束に用いる有職文様となりました。サナギから蝶に生まれ変わる神秘性は、不死不滅への願いから武士たちにも好んで使われました。

Butterfly patterns were introduced from China in the seventh century, and in the Heian era became court patterns used on the robes of nobles. The mysterious rebirth of the chrysalis as a butterfly made this a popular pattern among samurai, who desired immortality.

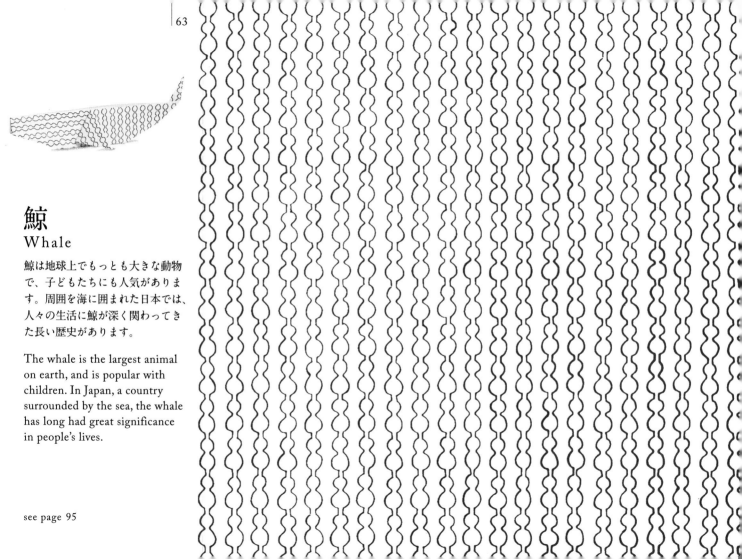

鯨
Whale

鯨は地球上でもっとも大きな動物
で、子どもたちにも人気がありま
す。周囲を海に囲まれた日本では、
人々の生活に鯨が深く関わってき
た長い歴史があります。

The whale is the largest animal
on earth, and is popular with
children. In Japan, a country
surrounded by the sea, the whale
has long had great significance
in people's lives.

see page 95

瓢箪立涌
ひょうたん

Hyotan-tatewaku

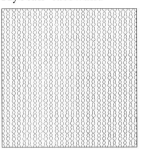

「立涌」の独特の曲線を「瓢箪」に見立
てた文様です。江戸時代には、このよ
うに伝統文様をアレンジしたものをは
じめ、遊び心のあるユニークな文様が
たくさんつくられました。

In this pattern the characteristic
curved lines of the *tatewaku*
(steam) motif have been shaped
into gourds. In the Edo era, many
playful and unique patterns were
created from traditional patterns.

折り方の基本形
Basic Shapes

本書で紹介している作品には、途中まで同じ折り方をするものがいくつかあります。よく出てくる折り方を「基本形1」「基本形2」としてここで説明します。

A number of the origami models introduced in this book are partially folded in the same way. Folds that are often used are explained here as "basic shape 1" and "basic shape 2".

基本形1
Basic Shape 1

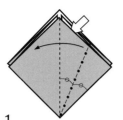

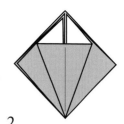

1

「四角折り」(15ページ) からはじめる。かどが開いているほうを上にする。ひだに折りすじをつけて、開いて、つぶす

Begin with the square base (page 15), with the open corners up. Crease the flap, open, and squash.

2

このように折る。残りの3つのひだも同じに

Fold like this. Repeat with the remaining three flaps.

3

「基本形1」のできあがり

Finished!

◎菖蒲 (74ページ)、花たとう (78ページ)、お化け (80ページ) はこの形からはじめます

The *ayame* (page 74), *hana-tato* (page 78) and ghost (page 80) are made from this shape.

基本形2
Basic Shape 2

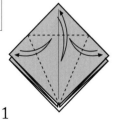

1

「四角折り」からはじめる。かどが開いているほうを下にする。真ん中の線に合わせて折りすじをつける

Begin with the square base, with the open corners down. Fold to the centerline to make creases.

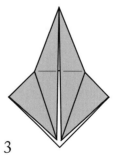

2

上の1枚を開き、折り線を使って矢印のほうへ折る

Open the upper layer and fold along the creases as shown.

3

折ったところ。うらも同じに

Make this shape. Repeat on the back.

4

「基本形2」のできあがり

Finished!

◎御駕篭 (76ページ)、燕 (84ページ) はこの形からはじめます

The *okago* (page 76) and swallow (page 84) are made from this shape.

足付き三方 Sanbo [see page 17]

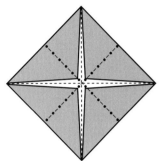

1

「ざぶとん折り」（16ページ）からはじめる。折りすじをつけて「四角折り」（15ページ）をする

Begin with the blintz base (page 16). Make creases and make into a square base (page 15).

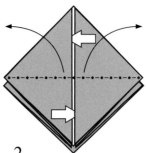

2

左右の三角を開いて、上に四角い袋を作るように折る

Open the left and right triangles, and make a rectangular pocket at the top.

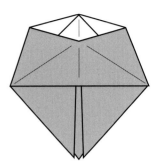

3

途中の図

In progress

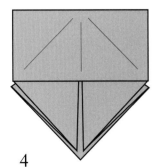

4

折ったところ。うらも同じに

Make this shape. Repeat on the back.

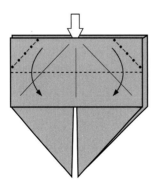

5

折りすじをつけ、四角の袋を開いて点線にそって折る

Make the creases shown, open the rectangular pocket, and fold along the dotted line.

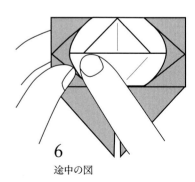

6

途中の図

In progress

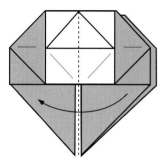

7

うらも同じに折り、上の1枚
を左に半分に折る。うらも同
じに

Repeat on the back, and
fold the upper flap to the
left. Repeat on the back.

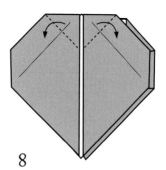

8

点線にそってかどを三角に折
る。うらも同じに

Fold the corners into triangles
along the dotted lines. Repeat
on the back.

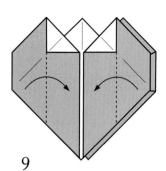

9

点線で折る。うらも同じに
Fold along the dotted lines.
Repeat on the back.

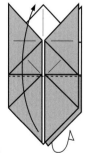

10

点線で半分に折る。うらも同
じに

Fold in half along the dotted
line. Repeat on the back.

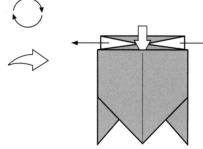

11

真ん中に指を入れて矢印の方
向に開く

Insert fingers in the center,
and open in the direction of
the arrows.

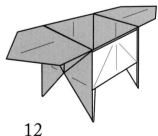

12

形をととのえて、できあがり
Adjust the shape. Finished!

奴さん Yakko-san [see page 19]

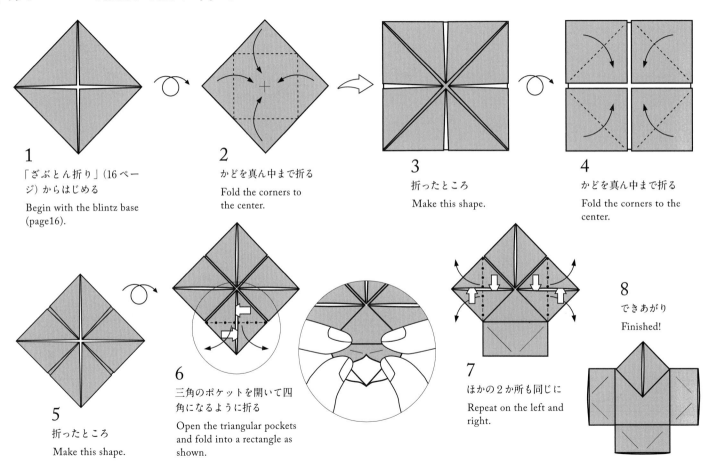

1

「ざぶとん折り」(16 ペー
ジ) からはじめる

Begin with the blintz base
(page16).

2

かどを真ん中まで折る

Fold the corners to
the center.

3

折ったところ

Make this shape.

4

かどを真ん中まで折る

Fold the corners to the
center.

5

折ったところ

Make this shape.

6

三角のポケットを開いて四
角になるように折る

Open the triangular pockets
and fold into a rectangle as
shown.

7

ほかの 2 か所も同じに

Repeat on the left and
right.

8

できあがり

Finished!

袴 Hakama [see page 21]

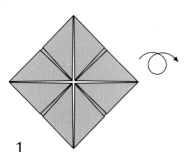

1

「奴さん」の5からはじめる

Begin from step 5 of the *yakko-san*.

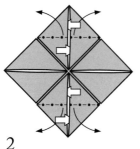

2

上下の三角のポケットを開いて四角になるように折る

On the top and bottom, open the triangular pockets and fold into rectangles.

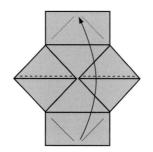

3

上に半分に折る

Fold in half towards the top.

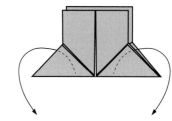

4

上部を開いて、左右の三角の内側の紙を引き出す

Open from the top, and pull out the inner triangular flaps.

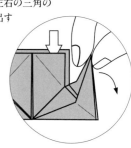

5

引き出したら矢印のところを押すようにして、「かぶせ折り」(15ページ)をする

Push at the arrow and make an outside reverse fold (page 15).

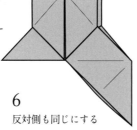

6

反対側も同じにする

Repeat on the left side.

7

できあがり

Finished!

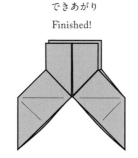

遊び方：奴さんに袴をはかせましょう。紙の間にはさんで、のり付けします

You can put the *hakama* on the *yakko-san*. Place between the flaps and glue.

手裏剣 Shuriken [see page 23] ✂

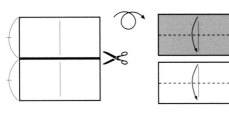

1
たて半分に折りすじをつけ
てから、真ん中で切る

Make a vertical crease.
Cut in half horizontally.

2
1枚はうらがえして、それ
ぞれ半分に折る

Turn over one flap, and
fold both in half.

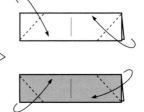

3
折ったところ

Male these shapes.

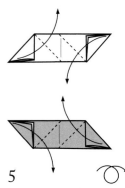

4
A・Bとも点線で折る

Fold A and B as shown
along the dotted lines.

5
A・Bとも点線で折る

Fold A and B as shown
along the dotted lines.

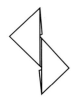

6
A 折ったところ

A will look like this.

B 折ってうら
がえしたところ

After folding and
turning over, B
will look like this.

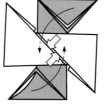

7
Aの向きを変えてBの上
に重ね、図のようにBを
Aに差しこむ

Change the direction of A,
place over B, and insert the
corners of B as shown.

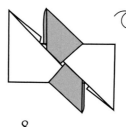

8
差しこんだところ

It will look like this.

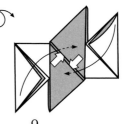

9
7と同様に差しこむ

Insert corners as in step 7.

10
できあがり

Finished!

鳩 Dove [see page 25]

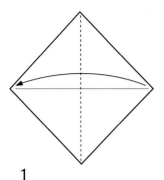

1

折りすじをつけ、半分に折る

Make a crease and fold in half.

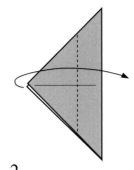

2

3分の1くらいのところで2枚とも折る

Fold both flaps over at about the 1/3 mark.

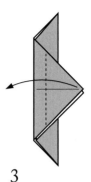

3

上の1枚を折る

Fold the top flap.

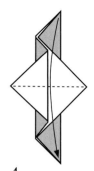

4

点線で半分に折る

Fold in half along the dotted line.

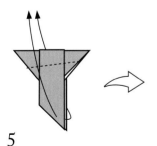

5

羽を斜めに折り上げる

Fold the wings up diagonally.

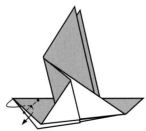

6

頭を「中わり折り」（15ページ）する

Make the head with an inside reverse fold (page 15).

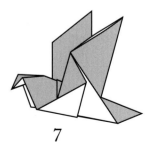

7

できあがり

Finished!

椿 Camellia [see page 27]

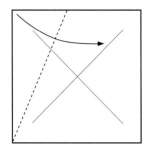

1

対角線に折りすじをつけ、真ん中の線に合うようにかどを折る

Make diagonal creases as shown, and fold the upper corner to the centerline.

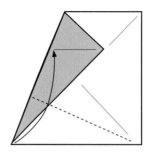

2

下のかどを真ん中の線に合うように折る

Fold the bottom corner to the centerline.

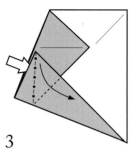

3

折りすじをつけて、間を開いて、上の1枚のみ矢印のほうへ折る

Make the crease shown. Open the flap and fold in the direction of the arrow.

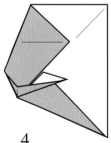

4

3の途中

Step 3 in progress.

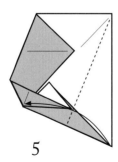

5

点線で折る

Fold along the dotted line.

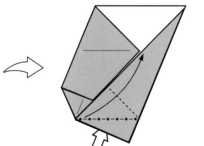

6

3と同じように折る

Fold as in step 3.

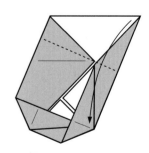

7

点線で折る

Fold along the dotted line.

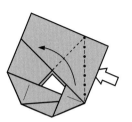

8

3と同じように折る

Fold as in step 3.

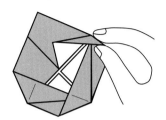

9

8の途中

Step 8 in progress.

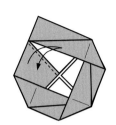

10

折りすじをつけて戻す

Make a crease and unfold.

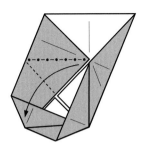

11

7、8で折ったところを上に
ひろげて点線で折る

Open the top and fold along
the dotted line.

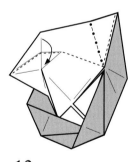

12

点線のとおりに、中にたたむ
ように折る

Fold along the dotted lines as
shown.

13

かどを下へさしこむ

Insert the corner in
the bottom.

14

内側のかどを小さく折る

Make small folds on the
inner corners.

15

できあがり

Finished!

菖蒲 Ayame [see page 29]

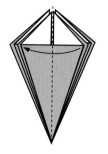

1

「基本形１」（65 ページ）から
はじめる。上の１枚を左へた
おす。うらも同じに

Begin with basic shape 1
(page 65). Push the upper
flap to the left. Repeat on
the back.

2

折ったところ

Make this shape.

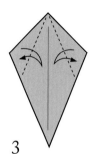

3

折りすじをつける

Make the creases shown.

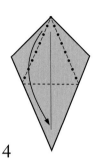

4

上の１枚を点線で折る

Fold the upper flap
down along the dotted
line.

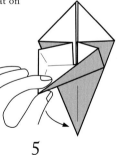

5

４の途中

Step 4 in progress.

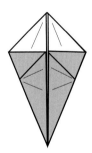

6

折ったところ。ほかの３か所
も同じに

Make this shape. Repeat with
the other three flaps.

7

上の１枚を点線で上に折る

Fold the upper flap up
along the dotted line.

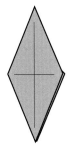

8

折ったところ。ほかの３か所
も同じに

Make this shape. Repeat with
the other three flaps.

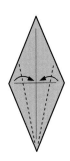

9

真ん中の線に合わせて折る

Fold to the centerline.

10

折ったところ。ほかの３か所
も同じに

Make this shape. Repeat with
the other three flaps.

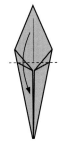

11

上の１枚を点線で下に折る

Fold the upper flap down
along the dotted line.

12

折ったところ。ほかの３か所
も同じに

Make this shape. Repeat with
the other three flaps.

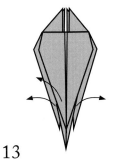

13

折り曲げた先の部分を上にひ
らく

Bring up the folded down
tips.

先をボールペンなどで
まくと丸みがつきます

Fold around a ballpoint
pen to round.

14

形をととのえて、できあがり

Adjust the shape. Finished!

御駕篭 Okago [see page 31]

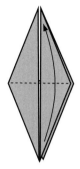

1

「基本形2」(65ページ)から
はじめる。かどが開いている
ほうを上にしておく。点線で
上に折る。うらも同じに

Begin with basic shape 2 (page 65), with the open corners up. Fold up along the dotted line. Repeat on the back.

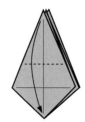

2

上の1枚を折る。うらも同じに

Fold the upper flap down. Repeat on the back.

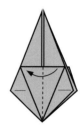

3

上の1枚を左に折る。うらも
同じに

Fold the upper flap to the left. Repeat on the back.

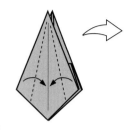

4

真ん中に合わせて折る。うら
も同じに

Fold to the centerline. Repeat on the back.

5

三角のポケットをよこに開い
て図6のようにする。うらも
同じに

Open the triangular pockets horizontally as in step 6. Repeat on the back.

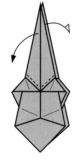

6

とんがり2本をそれぞれ手前
に折る

Fold the two sharp points towards yourself.

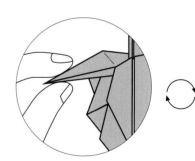

6の途中。横から見たところ

Step 6 in progress, as seen from the side.

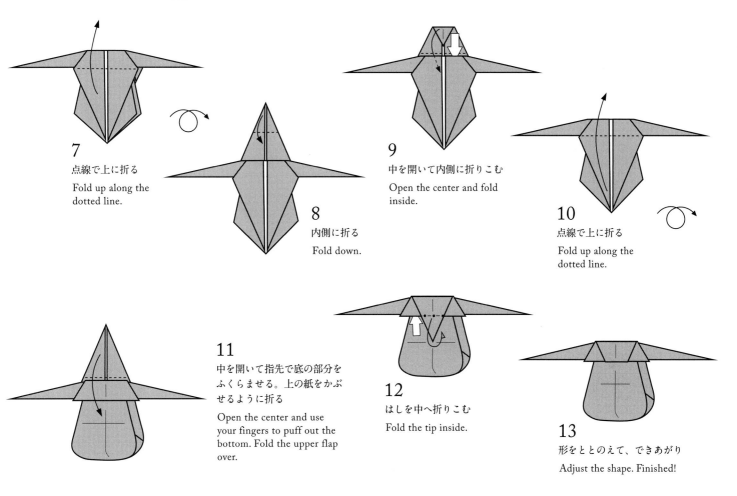

7

点線で上に折る

Fold up along the dotted line.

8

内側に折る

Fold down.

9

中を開いて内側に折りこむ

Open the center and fold inside.

10

点線で上に折る

Fold up along the dotted line.

11

中を開いて指先で底の部分をふくらませる。上の紙をかぶせるように折る

Open the center and use your fingers to puff out the bottom. Fold the upper flap over.

12

はしを中へ折りこむ

Fold the tip inside.

13

形をととのえて、できあがり

Adjust the shape. Finished!

花たとう Hana-tato [see page 33]

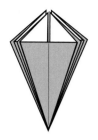

1

「基本形1」（65ページ）から
はじめる。ここまで折ったら
全体を開く

Begin with basic shape 1 (page
65). After folding, unfold.

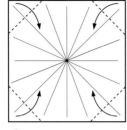

2

かどを図のように折る

Fold the corners as shown.

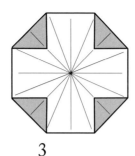

3

折ったところ

Make this shape.

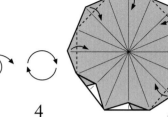

4

かどを図のように折る（8か
所）

Fold the corners as shown
(all eight).

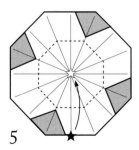

5

★が☆（中心）につくように
折る

Fold so the ★ meets the ☆
(center).

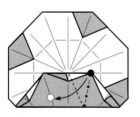

6

●が○につくように折る

Fold so the ● meets
the ○.

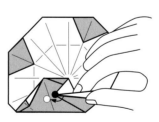

7

6の途中の図。5～7をほか
の7か所でくり返す

Step 6 in progress. Repeat
steps 5 to 7 with the other
seven corners.

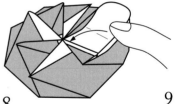

8

最初にたたんだところを開き、
最後のほうをたたんで最初の
下に入れる

Open the first corner, and
fold the last corner under
the first.

9

できあがり
Finished!

狐の面 Fox Mask [see page 35]

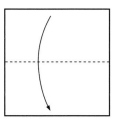

1
半分に折る
Fold in half.

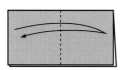

2
折りすじをつける
Make a crease.

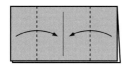

3
真ん中に合わせて折る
Fold to the center.

4
四角の部分を開き、三角を作るように折る
Open the rectangles, and fold into triangles.

4の途中。
Step 4 in progress.

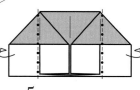

5
両はしを後ろへ折る
Fold both edges back.

6
折ったところ
Make this shape.

7
上の1枚を点線で折る
Fold the upper flap along the dotted line.

8
上の1枚を点線で折る。うらも7、8を同様にする
Fold the upper flap along the dotted line. Fold the back as in steps 7 and 8.

9
中を開く
Open the center.

10
上下に指を入れて口の部分をへこませる
Insert fingers in the top and bottom, and collapse the mouth.

11
できあがり
Finished!

遊び方：指で口をパクパクさせて遊びます
Make her open and close her mouth with your fingers!

お化け Ghost [see page 37] ✂

1

「基本形1」(65ページ)から
はじめる。かどが開いてい
るほうを下にする。両はしを
折って折りすじをつける

Begin with basic shape 1
(page 65), with the open
corners down. Make creases
on both sides.

2

三角の袋を開き、点線で折る

Open the triangular pocket
and fold along the dotted
lines.

3

折ったところ。ほかの3か所
も1〜3を同様にする

Make this shape. Fold the other
three pockets as in steps 1 to 3.

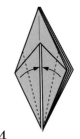

4

上の1枚を内側に折る

Fold the upper flaps
to the centerline.

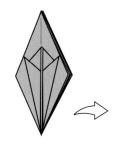

5

折ったところ。ほかの3か所
も同じに

Make this shape. Repeat
with the other three flaps.

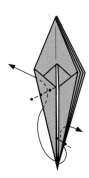

6

点線にそって腕と足を「中わ
り折り」(15ページ)する。う
らも同じに

Make inside reverse folds
(page 15) for the arms and
legs along the dotted lines.

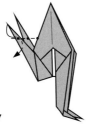

7

手の先を「中わり折り」する(紙
がかたくて折れないときは内
側に折る)

Make inside reverse folds for
the hands (if the paper is too
stiff, just fold in).

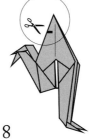

8

はさみで水平に切り込みを入
れる。切ったところを上に引
き出す

Make a horizontal cut with
scissors. Pull the cut portion
up and out.

9

できあがり

Finished!

雉 Pheasant [see page 39] ✂

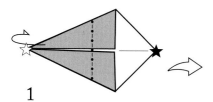

1

「凧折り」(16ページ)からは
じめる。山折りして、☆と★
を合わせる

Begin with the kite base (page
16). Make a mountain fold so
the ☆ meets the ★.

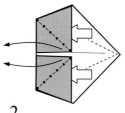

2

図のように折りすじをつけ、
左に引き出すように折る

Make the creases as shown,
and pull out and fold to the
left.

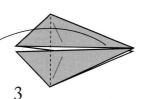

3

上の1枚を点線で折る

Fold the upper flap along the
dotted line.

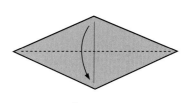

4

半分に折る

Fold in half.

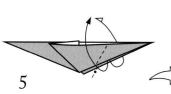

5

「かぶせ折り」(15ページ)して
首の部分を作る

Make the neck with an
outside reverse fold (page 15).

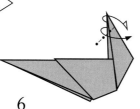

6

「かぶせ折り」で頭を作る

Make the head with an
outside reverse fold.

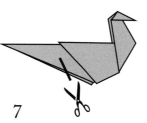

7

紙の途中まで、はさみで斜め
に切り込みを入れる

Make a diagonal cut halfway
into the paper with scissors.

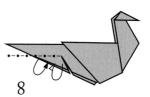

8

かどを内側に折りこむ

Fold the corners in.

9

できあがり
Finished!

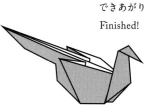

相撲取り Sumo Wrestler [see page 41]

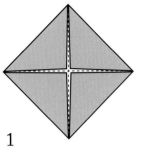

1

「ざぶとん折り」(16 ページ)からはじめて、折りすじをつける

Begin with the blintz base (page 16), and make the creases shown.

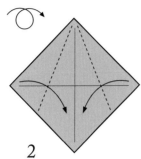

2

真ん中に合わせて折る

Fold to the centerline.

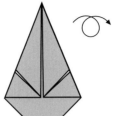

3

折ったところ

Make this shape.

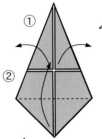

4

①は左右に開く。
②は点線で折る

Open ① out and fold ② up.

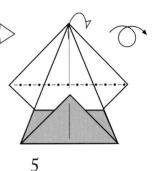

5

点線で山折りする

Make a mountain fold along the dotted line.

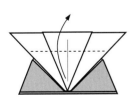

6

上の１枚のみ点線で折る

Fold the upper flap up along the dotted line.

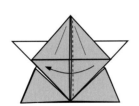

7

全体を半分に折る

Fold in half.

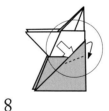

8

背中のところを開き、「かぶせ折り」(15 ページ)で「まわし」を作る

Open the lower back, and make a *mawashi* (wrestler's belt) with an outside reverse fold (page 15).

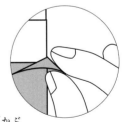

9

できあがり

Finished!

渡し舟 Ferryboat [see page 43]

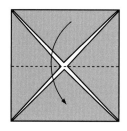

1

「ざぶとん折り」(16ページ)
から半分に折る

Begin with the blintz base
(page 16) and fold in half.

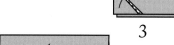

2

半分に折る。以下2〜6まで
うらも同じにする

Fold in half. Repeat steps
2 to 6 on the back.

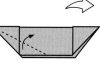

3

かどを折る

Fold the corners.

4

かどを折る

Fold the corner.

5

かどを折る

Fold the corner.

6

かどを折る。紙が固くなって
折りにくいので注意

Fold the corner. Take care
as the paper will be stiff and
difficult to fold.

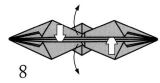

7

折ったところ

Make this
shape.

8

7を上から見た図。矢印のと
ころから開く

Step 7 as seen from above.
Open as shown by the arrows.

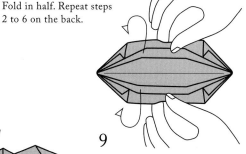

9

真ん中をひろげたら、紙を破
らないように気をつけながら、
全体をうら返す（袋をうら返
すように）

After opening the center,
taking care not to rip the paper,
flip everything inside out (as if
turning a bag inside out).

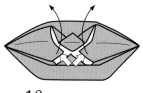

10

かどを上に持ち上げる

Bring the corners to
the top.

11

はしを内側へ折りこむ

Fold the tips in.

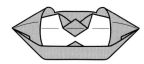

12

形をととのえて、できあがり

Adjust the shape. Finished!

ピアノ Piano [see page 45]

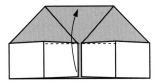

1

「狐の面」（79 ページ）の5からはじめる。前の部分を上に折る

Begin from step 5 of the fox mask (page 79). Fold the front flap up.

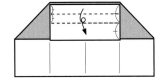

2

点線でまくように折る（鍵盤を作る）

Fold up along the dotted lines as if rolling up (make the keyboard).

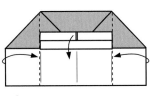

3

両はしを内側へ折り、鍵盤のところを下げる

Fold both edges in, and fold the keyboard down.

4

鍵盤を水平にして立たせる

Make the keyboard horizontal, and stand up.

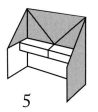

5

できあがり

Finished!

燕 Swallow [see page 47] ✂

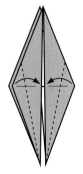

1

「基本形2」（65 ページ）からはじめる。真ん中の線に合わせて折る。うらも同じに

Begin with basic shape 2 (page 65). Fold the edges in to the centerline. Repeat on the back.

2

上の1枚のみ左へたおす。うらも同じに

Fold over the top flap only. Repeat on the back.

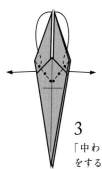

3
「中わり折り」（15 ページ）
をする

Make inside reverse folds
(page 15).

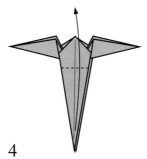

4
上の 1 枚のみ点線で折り上げる

Fold the upper flap only up
along the dotted line.

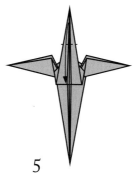

5
先を下に折る

Fold the tip down.

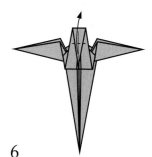

6
先端が少しとびでるように折る

Fold the tip so it sticks out a
little.

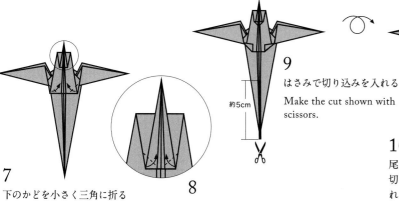

7
下のかどを小さく三角に折る

Fold the bottom corners
into small triangles.

8
図のようにかどを折る

Fold the corners as in the
diagram.

9
はさみで切り込みを入れる

Make the cut shown with
scissors.

約5cm

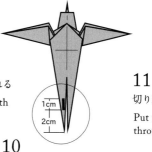

10
尾のところにカッターなどで
切り込み（約1センチ）を入
れる

Use a box cutter etc. to make
a small cut in the tail (about
1 cm).

1cm
2cm

11
切り込みに反対側の先を通す

Put the tip of the opposite side
through the cut.

12
できあがり

Finished!

祝い包み Iwai-zutsumi [see pages 49]

アレンジ／中島 進
Arranged by Susumu Nakajima

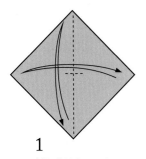

1

折りすじをつける

Make creases as shown.

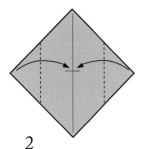

2

真ん中に合わせて折る

Fold to the centerline.

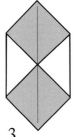

3

折ったところ

Make this shape.

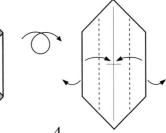

4

真ん中に合わせて折る（うら
の三角は折らない）

Fold to the centerline
(don't fold the back
triangles).

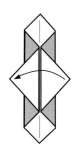

5

上の1枚を左に合わせる

Fold the upper flap to meet
the left.

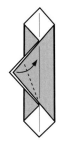

6

上の1枚のみ点線で折る

Fold the upper flap only
along the crease.

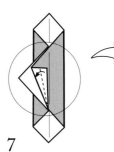

7

さらに半分に折る

Fold in half again.

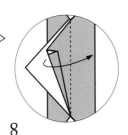

8

上の1枚のみ点線で折る

Fold the upper flap only
along the dotted line.

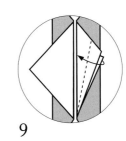

9

まとめて点線で折る

Fold along the dotted line.

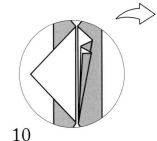

10

折ったところ。左側も6〜9
まで同様に

Make this shape. Repeat
steps 6 to 9 on the left.

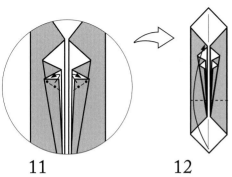

11

小さく内側に折る

Make small folds
to the inside.

12

点線で上に折る

Fold up along
the dotted line.

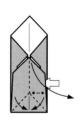

13

上の1枚のみ折りすじをつける

Make creases on the upper
flap only.

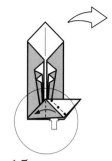

14

間を開いてたたむ（図15参照）

Open the middle and fold as
shown (see step 15).

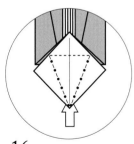

15

間を開いてたたむ

Open the middle
and fold over.

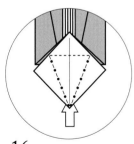

16

間を開いて上に折り上げる

Open the middle and
fold up.

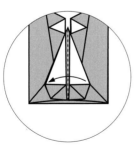

17

図の位置を半分に折る

Fold in half as shown.

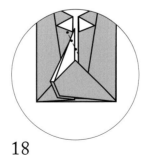

18

「中わり折り」（15ページ）を
してツルの頭を作る

Make the crane's head with an
inside reverse fold (page 15).

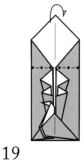

19

点線で山折りする

Make a mountain fold
along the dotted line.

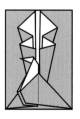

20

できあがり

Finished!

鷹 Hawk [see page 51]

1

「お化け」（80 ページ）の 4
からはじめる（上下を逆に）。
上の 1 枚を左にたおす

Begin from step 4 of the
ghost (page 80). Turn upside
down. Fold the top flap to
the left.

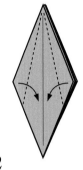

2

真ん中に合わせて折る

Fold to the centerline.

3

上の 1 枚を右へたおす

Fold the top flap to the right.

4

上の 1 枚を右へたおす

Fold the top flap to the right.

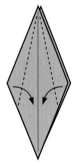

5

真ん中に合わせて折る

Fold to the centerline.

6

上の 1 枚を左にたおす

Fold the top layer to the left.

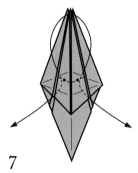

7

前のとんがり 2 本を「中わり
折り」（15 ページ）する

Inside reverse fold (page 15)
the two front points.

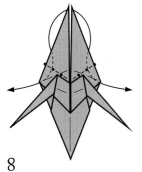

8

うしろのとんがり2本を「中
わり折り」する（7と方向を
ずらして）

Inside reverse fold the two
back points (in a different
direction from step 7).

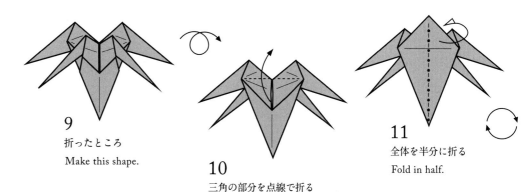

9

折ったところ

Make this shape.

10

三角の部分を点線で折る

Fold the triangle up along
the dotted line.

11

全体を半分に折る

Fold in half.

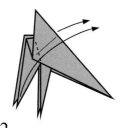

12

点線で折って羽を作る。うら
も同じに

Fold along the dotted line to
make a wing. Repeat on the
back.

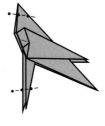

13

くちばしと足を「中わり折
り」する

Make inside reverse folds for
the beak and feet.

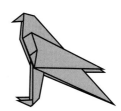

14

できあがり

Finished!

提灯 Chochin [see page 53]

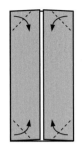

1

「かんのん折り」（16 ページ）
から始める。かどを点線で折る

Begin with a kannon fold (page
16). Fold the corners along the
dotted lines.

2

上と下を山折りする

Mountain fold the top
and bottom.

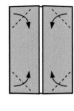

3

かどを点線で折る

Fold the corners along
the dotted lines.

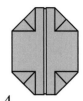

4

折ったところ

Make this shape.

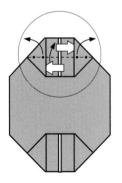

5

三角のポケットを開いて四角
になるように折る

Open the triangular pockets
and fold into a rectangle.

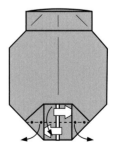

6

下も 5 と同様に折る

Repeat step 5 on the
bottom.

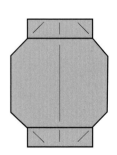

7

できあがり

Finished!

蝸牛 Snail [see page 55] ✂

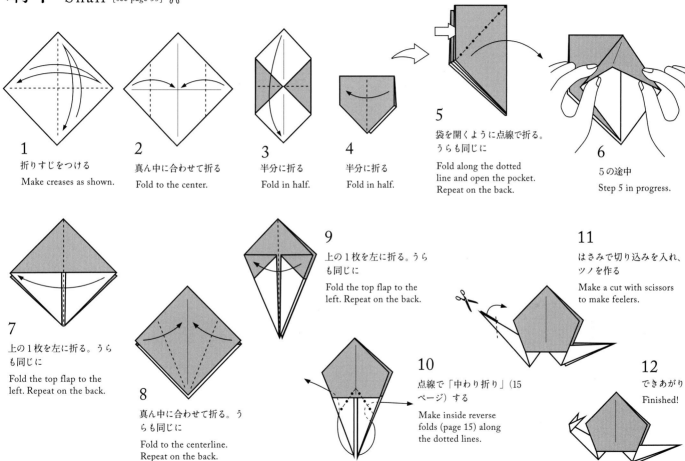

1
折りすじをつける
Make creases as shown.

2
真ん中に合わせて折る
Fold to the center.

3
半分に折る
Fold in half.

4
半分に折る
Fold in half.

5
袋を開くように点線で折る。
うらも同じに
Fold along the dotted line and open the pocket. Repeat on the back.

6
5の途中
Step 5 in progress.

7
上の1枚を左に折る。うら
も同じに
Fold the top flap to the left. Repeat on the back.

8
真ん中に合わせて折る。う
らも同じに
Fold to the centerline. Repeat on the back.

9
上の1枚を左に折る。うら
も同じに
Fold the top flap to the left. Repeat on the back.

10
点線で「中わり折り」（15
ページ）する
Make inside reverse folds (page 15) along the dotted lines.

11
はさみで切り込みを入れ、
ツノを作る
Make a cut with scissors to make feelers.

12
できあがり
Finished!

蝉 Cicada [see page 57]

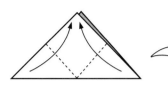

1

表を内側にして三角に折り、
点線で折る

Fold into a triangle with the colored side in and fold along the creases.

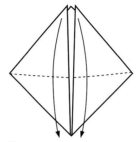

2

すこし斜めに折り下げる

Fold down on a slight diagonal.

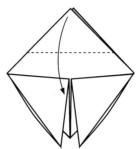

3

上の1枚を半分よりやや下の
線で折る

Fold the upper flap down a little below the centerline.

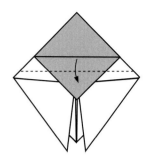

4

もう一度折る

Fold again.

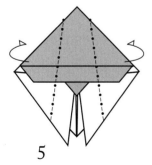

5

斜めに山折りする

Make diagonal mountain folds.

6

山折りして頭を作る

Make the head with a mountain fold.

7

かどを小さく折る

Make small folds on the corners.

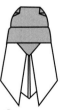

8

できあがり

Finished!

豚 Pig [see page 59]

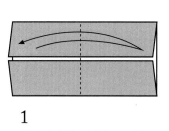

1

「かんのん折り」（16 ページ）
からはじめる。半分に折りす
じをつける

Begin with a double parallel
fold (page 16). Make a crease
in the middle.

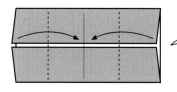

2

真ん中に合わせて折る

Fold to the centerline.

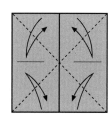

3

上の 1 枚のみ折りすじをつ
ける

Make creases as shown
(upper flaps).

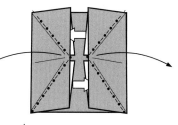

4

開いて上下に三角を作るよう
に折る

Open and fold to make triangles
on the top and bottom.

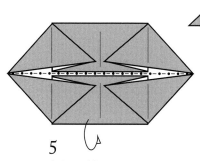

5

半分に山折りする

Fold in half with a
mountain fold.

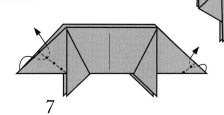

6

点線で折って足を作る。うら
も同じに

Fold along the dotted lines
to make legs. Repeat on the
back.

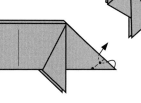

7

「中わり折り」（15 ページ）し
てハナとしっぽを作る

Make the nose and tail with
inside reverse folds (page 15).

8

できあがり

Finished!

帽子 Hat(Sombrero) [see page 61]

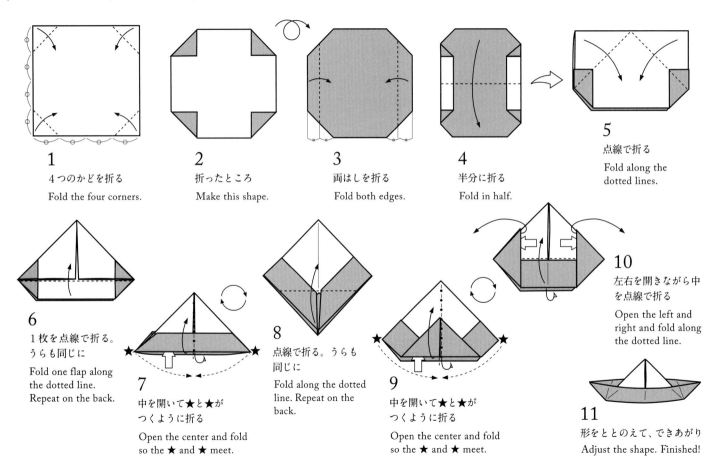

1

4つのかどを折る

Fold the four corners.

2

折ったところ

Make this shape.

3

両はしを折る

Fold both edges.

4

半分に折る

Fold in half.

5

点線で折る

Fold along the dotted lines.

6

1枚を点線で折る。
うらも同じに

Fold one flap along the dotted line. Repeat on the back.

7

中を開いて★と★が
つくように折る

Open the center and fold so the ★ and ★ meet.

8

点線で折る。うらも
同じに

Fold along the dotted line. Repeat on the back.

9

中を開いて★と★が
つくように折る

Open the center and fold so the ★ and ★ meet.

10

左右を開きながら中
を点線で折る

Open the left and right and fold along the dotted line.

11

形をととのえて、できあがり

Adjust the shape. Finished!

鯨 Whale [see page 63]

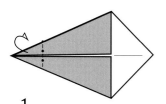

1

「凧折り」(16ページ)からは
じめる。点線で山折りする

Begin with the kite base (page
16). Make a mountain fold
along the dotted line.

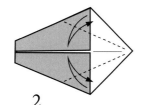

2

折りすじをつける

Make creases.

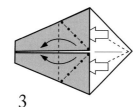

3

中を開いて点線で折る

Open both sides and fold
along the dotted lines.

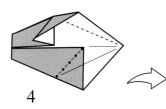

4

3の途中

Step 3 in progress.

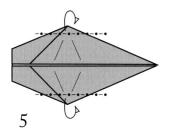

5

点線で山折りする

Make mountain folds along
the dotted lines.

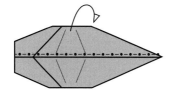

6

全体を半分に折る

Fold in half.

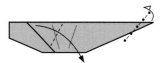

7

点線で折って胸ビレ(うらも)
と尾を作る

Fold along the dotted lines
to make the pectoral fins and
the tail.

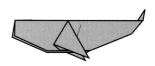

8

できあがり

Finished!

監修——小林一夫

1941年東京生まれ。内閣府認証NPO法人国際おりがみ協会理事長。お茶の水・おりがみ会館館長。全国の折り紙教室で指導や講演を行うかたわら、世界各国で折り紙や和紙を通じた国際交流、日本文化の紹介活動を行っている。著書多数。

Editorial Supervisor——Kazuo Kobayashi

Kazuo Kobayashi is the chairman of the International Origami Association (an incorporated nonprofit organization) and director of the Origami Center in Ochanomizu. He was born in Tokyo in 1941. He teaches and lectures origami classes all over Japan. He also organizes programs that use *washi* and origami to foster international exchange and introduce Japanese culture around the world. He has published many books about origami.

編集——宮下　真 (オフィスM2)
アートディレクション——有山達也
デザイン——池田千草 (アリヤマデザインストア)
撮影——石川美香
千代紙スタイリング——田中美和子
作品制作・折り図作成——湯浅信江
英訳—— Sarah McNally
協力——伊澤悠紀子
折り図トレース——株式会社エストール

千代紙・撮影協力——「ゆしまの小林」
　　　　　　　　　お茶の水・おりがみ会館
　　　　　　　　　URL http://www.origamikaikan.co.jp/
参考文献————『日本の文様』(小林一夫著・日本ヴォーグ社)
　　　　　　　『日本・中国の文様事典』(視覚デザイン研究所)
　　　　　　　『すぐわかる日本の伝統文様』(東京美術)

英訳付き　伝承折り紙帖

監修者　小林一夫
発行者　池田　豊
印刷所　図書印刷株式会社
製本所　図書印刷株式会社
発行所　株式会社池田書店
　　　　東京都新宿区弁天町43番地 (〒162-0851)
　　　　☎ 03-3267-6821 (代)／振替 00120-9-60072
　　　　落丁、乱丁はお取り替えいたします。

©K. K. Ikeda Shoten 2007, Printed in Japan
ISBN978-4-262-15250-9

0700009